North Korea

A Look Into The World's Most Mysterious Country

Table of Contents

Introduction

You are probably intrigued with North Korea as it's always making headlines for terrifying reasons. For example, it has made numerous threats to blow up South Korea, the USA, and its allies.

Another issue that draws attention is its disreputable human rights record. In addition, despite devoting a huge part of its national income to its military, the country is poverty stricken, though things are starting to improve.

However, North Korean broadcasts and messages to the world are not in line with any of the above. And this confuses many. The country depicts itself as a heaven, with all the citizens happy and rallying their leader to unleash more horror to the world. If it isn't a verbal or physical fight with South Korea, then it's a threat to the USA.

In this book, we will look are the history of North Korea. The journey will begin with how the country came into existence. Then we will move on to how one family has ruled it for more than 60 years.

Since nuclear terror is among North Korea's biggest controversies, we won't forget to peek into how the program started and what its motives are.

I hope you will enjoy the reading. Let's get started!

Chapter 1: The Birth of North Korea

North and South Korea used to be one country. The curse that led to their split started in 1910 when Japan took over the country following the Japan-Korea Annexation Treaty.

Under Japan's control, Koreans lived in misery. They were made to work in farms, taken as slaves, and forced to fight for Japan. Those who resisted were persecuted. Japan was determined to end Korea that it established several laws that hindered the survival of Korean culture. Even schools weren't allowed to teach the Korean language.

Owing to the state of affairs, several Koreans formed guerrilla groups to fight

Japan. In 1919, they held nationwide Independence rallies. Japan responded with brutal force, resulting in the death of 7,000 peaceful demonstrators.

In the face of pressure, from both Koreans and the international community, Japan made reforms aimed at giving the Koreans some freedom. But the situation didn't improve.

At the Cairo conference on 22 November 1943, China, Britain, and the USA agreed that Japan had to be stripped of all its colonies. This included giving Korea independence.

The post-war planners agreed that after Japan's defeat in WWII, the Soviets would control the northern part of Korea while the US would take the south. This was a short-term administrative measure; Korea would be unified at a later date.

Japan surrendered to the Allied forces on 15 August in 1945. And as agreed, Soviet Union took control of the northern part. Its tanks entered the Korean Peninsula on August 9, 1945. Since Japan had not surrendered yet, the tanks met some resistance.

US troops landed in the southern part in September. With Japan gone, another problem arose: the Soviets wanted Korea to be a communist regime, not the democratic government the US had proposed.

Several talks failed to establish a common ground between the two parties. And in 1947, USA submitted the matter to the UN General Assembly. The UN issued a mandate ordering the Soviet Union to not block democratic elections in Korea. But the Soviets ignored the UN mandate.

With Soviet's noncooperation, the US went ahead with democratic elections in the South, and Syngman Rhee emerged as the winner. This made him the leader of the newly founded Republic of Korea (ROK), commonly known as South Korea.

The Soviets also went on and installed Kim Il-sung as the leader of the Democratic People's Republic of Korea (DPRK), popularly known as North Korea. This meant a communist dictatorship ruled the North and a democratic government controlled the South. On December 12, 1948, the UN recognized the Republic of Korea as the sole government of Korea. Under a UN agreement, the Soviet Union and USA withdrew their soldiers from North and South Korea respectively. Only advisers were left behind.

The Korean War

After the establishment of governments in North and South Korea, tensions continued to rise. On June 25, 1950, 75,000 soldiers from the North Korean People's Army crossed the 38th parallel, an imaginary line dividing the two countries, marking the beginning of the Korean War.

During this time, South Korea was going through hardships and failed to defend itself. The North Koreans exploited this and managed to claim a good part of the country.

The UN sent troops in July, dominated by U.S forces, to help South Korea. Within months, the UN forces regained much of what the North Koreans had taken. And they also managed to push their rivals past beyond the 38th parallel.

With the UN forces with the edge, the decision gravitated towards going on to conquer North Korea and not stop at the 38th parallel. But before that decision would be exercised, China got behind North Korea's back, increasing fears for WWIII. As a result, the UN forces retreated to the 38th parallel.

The war ended in stalemate in July 1953. This meant the situation had returned to its status before the war. The US and its allies had succeeded in stopping North Korea from making the South a communist country. And the Soviets had also succeeded in keeping the democratic government of the South from spreading into the North.

For the Koreans, it was a failure; they had failed to unify themselves. 5 million soldiers and civilians died with nothing good to show for it. Although the war ended, skirmishes along the 38th parallel continued.

Chapter 2: Kim Dynasty

Since the birth of North Korea, only 3 people have ruled it. These are the country's first president, his son, and now, his grandson. Despite the fall of the Soviet Union, North Korea hasn't changed its system of governance.

Kim Il-sung

Kim Il-sung was the first leader of North Korea after being installed on the post by the Soviet Union. His childhood is nothing but a mystery. Some claim the secrecy is done on purpose so that the North Korean officials can exaggerate his greatness.

From the data available, Kim Il-sung was born on 15 April 1912. He was an active member of the Korean guerrilla resistance against Japan in the 1930s. Soviet military authorities noticed his abilities and sent him to the Soviet Union for military and political training.

After the surrender of Japan in 1945, the Soviets wanted him as the leader of Korea. And in 1948, they made him the first prime minister of North Korea. He held the position until he became president in 1972. He remained president until his death in 1994.

Kim Il-sung was responsible for starting the Korean War. Under his rule, North Korea became a socialist state. This was largely influenced by the training he received in the Soviet Union.

Kim Il-sung developed a personality cult that strengthened his grip on power. He eliminated everyone who challenged, enabling him to run for 46 years without any opposition. Additionally, this cleared the way for his son to rule the country after him. Apart from his communist ideas, he was also famous for is his Juche philosophy: an idea that a country must survive on its own.

During Kim Il-sung's reign, North Korea's biggest allies were the Soviet Union and China. North Koreans refer to him as the Great Leader. It is believed that there are about 34,000 statues of him in the country. His birthday is a public holiday and it's called the Day of the Sun.

Kim Jong-il

Kim Il-sung started preparing his son, Kim Jong-il, to take over power long before 1980, mostly by giving him high profile positions in the government. It was officially made public in October 1980 that Kim Jong-il was the heir apparent.

And as planned, Kim Jong-il became the de facto leader of North Korea after his father's death in 1994. He was named chairman of the Korean Workers' Party in October 1997. He later ascended to the country's highest position in September 1998.

Just like his father, much is not known about Kim Jong-il's childhood. But according to North Korean sources, he was born in a guerrilla base camp on Mount Paektu. The story goes on to say his birth was foretold by a double rainbow that appeared in the sky. And a night star also appeared on the day of his birth. He was able to walk at 3 weeks and was talking by week 8.

Proving his greatness even further, he had the ability to control the weather through the power of thought.

But one thing we really know is that Kim Jong-il had a love for arts. He was mostly interested in making films.

Reports claim he was responsible for the abduction of South Korean firm director, Shi Sang-ok, and his actress wife, Choi Eun-hee, in the '70s. The motive for the abduction was to create a movie industry in North Korea. The two escaped in 1986 after years of being forced to make movies.

However, things took a surprise turn when North Korea's economy collapsed. Poverty rates increased and famine left many people dead. To ease the suffering on the people, Kim abandoned his father's Juche philosophy and formed relationships with several countries.

Furthermore, talks took place in hope of ending the tension with South Korea. Despite these new developments, the two countries continued to poke each other's throat.

Experts now agree that these newly formed relationships were nothing more than a means of getting aid. In 2008, rumors of Kim Jong-il's deteriorating healthy started surfacing. Some claimed he had suffered from stroke. On December 19, 2011, he was announced dead by North Korean state media, with heart attack as the cause of death.

Kim Jong-il was famously known as the Dear leader. This title later changed to Great General. Just like his father, his pictures are almost everywhere in the country.

Kim Jong-un

Kim Jong-un succeeded his father, Kim Jong-il, in 2011. It was made official in 2010 that he was next in line for power. But before this, he was given control of high profile positions in his father's government. He was even made a 4-star general despite his lack of military experience.

Nobody thought Kim Jong-un was to lead North Korea after his father. As such, analysts focused on his two elder brothers as potential candidates.

However, Kim Jong-un's half-brother, Kim Jong-nam, was deported from Japan for traveling to Disneyland on a forged passport. This squashed any chances of him being considered for leadership.

Kim Jong-un's other brother, Kim Jong-chol, was also passed as he is considered to be too feminine. Taking over power at 30 made Kim Jong-un the world's youngest serving state leader. Kim Jong-il's death was untimely as he was still grooming the young Kim for leadership.

Since ascending to power in 2011, Kim Jong-un has executed several high profile officials, including one who mentored him to power. Many of his victims were executed on grounds of trying to overthrow the government.

Many believe that since Kim is young, North Koreans doubt his leadership abilities. And the executions prove how insecure he is. Reports of his birth year contradict; some say it is 1983 while others insist that 1984 is correct.

Kim Jong-un is believed to have wed former cheerleader and singer, Ri Sol Ju, in 2009. It is also believed that he has a daughter. He is mainly interested in sports, especially basketball. And rumor has it that he is a big fan of American basketball legend Michael Jordan. Although he is wedded, he is known to be a womanizer.

Chapter 3: Inter-Korean Relationship

Based on the level of conflict between North and South Korea, one would doubt that there have been moments of peace between the two. But remember that they used to be one before Japan's surrendered to the Allied forces. Additionally, the war that increased their division was meant to unite.

Since the war, the relationship between the two Koreas has been full of ups and downs. Just after the war, both countries were busy restoring order in their respective nations. Since the wounds from that fight were yet to heal, there was hostility between the two that communication was almost non-existent.

Crashes in the DMZ continued right into the late 60s. And in an attempt to destabilize the South, the North tried to assassinate South Korean president, Park Chung-hee, in 1968.

But things took a positive turn in the early '70s following the reestablishment of relations between the US and China. The two Koreas saw it in their best interest to also start dialogue. But this new breath of hope did not make an impact.

In 1983, North Korea tried to assassinate then-president of South Korea, Chun Doo-hwan. This failed attempt made matters worse. Thankfully, negotiations went on, preventing what would have been another bloody situation.

From the talks, the two agreed to allow South and North Koreans who were split to reunite in Seoul and Pyongyang in 1985. But this wave of hope did not last long. In 1987, Korean Air Flight 858 was shot in the air.

Significant negotiations resumed under South Korea's new leader, Roh Tae-woo, who rose to power in 1988. He introduced the Nordpolitik Policy, which sought to establish relations with the Soviet Union and China.

The policy also enabled the first Inter-Korean trade in 1989 and other noteworthy changes. Compared with the previous years, this was a step in the right direction to seeking peace.

Roh was succeeded by Kim Young-sam in 1993, who promised a hardline approach to North Korea. In the same year, Pyongyang was accused of violating the Nonproliferation Treaty. And Seoul responded with the suspension of economic exchanges. At Kim Il-sung's death, the South did not send condolences.

Kim Dae Jung, who followed Kim Young-sam, brought some fresh hope to the North-South relationship. He introduced the Sunshine Policy aimed at facilitating reconciliation with his neighbor. The policy allowed businesses, NGOs, and private citizens from the two countries to have contact.

And when North Korea suffered from famine in 1998, Seoul provided assistance in food and fertilizer. The strengthened relationship led to the meeting of Kim Dae Jung and Kim Jong-il in June 2000 in Pyongyang for the first presidential summit. This marked the first time a South Korean leader met with one from the North.

At the summit, the two leaders agreed to resume family reunification meetings. They also agreed to establish Inter-Korean Kaesong Industrial Complex (KIC) near the DMZ. This was a symbol of their union despite their political differences. The Sunshine Policy made it that humanitarian and economic cooperation would continue amidst political tension. South Korea elected a new president, Roh Moo Hyun, in 2003. Just like his predecessor, he also focused on improving relations with his neighbor that he introduced the Policy for Peace and Prosperity.

Unfortunately, his wish for peace and prosperity did not materialize as North Korea was then strengthening its nuclear power. This meant it had violated several agreements it had made on keeping the Peninsula free from nuclear weapons.

As a result, South Korea was forced to reduce aid and temporarily suspended fertilizer and food shipment to North Korea. But this did not affect investment at KIC.

Roh met Kim Jong-il in 2007 at the second presidential summit. The two agreed on a number of projects aimed at strengthening their relationship. However, these projects were never followed through by the next regime of

Lee Myung Bak, which came to power in 2008. North Korea's nuclear program was advancing and Lee's policies focused on denuclearization.

By early 2009, the relationship between the two countries had deteriorated. And North Korea declared all past agreements with South Korea nullified. This led to increased tension between the two.

In March 2010, a South Korean corvette, the Cheonan, sank after an explosion killing 46 South Korean sailors. The blame was placed on North Korea as it was alleged that its submarine had shot the corvette.

This angered the South Koreans and Lee demanded an apology, which North Korea refused to give. Lee announced several new unilateral sanctions on North Korea. For the remainder of his term, the situation between the two remained tense.

Lee was succeeded by Park Geun Hye, Park Chung-hee's daughter, in December 2012. The new leader promised to focus on strengthening the economy and improving relations with North Korea. But she made it clear that she would respond to provocations forcefully.

Tensions hit a peak just after Park's inauguration. And it did not take long before North Korea declared it was in a state of war with South Korea. The North withdrew its 53,000 workers at KIC, forcing South Korea to follow suit.

However, talks resumed in the next few months.

Chapter 4: North Korea's Economy

Both North and South Korea were devastated after the war. And by the late '50s, they were both focused on improving their economies through industrialization.

The North was at an advantage as Japan had based most of its industrial investments on that side. Additionally, it had more natural resources than the South. Coupled with help from the Soviet Union and China, North Korea's economy expanded rapidly.

The country invested heavily in mining, buying dedicated machines from other countries. Much of this investment was financed by heavy borrowing. The plan was to repay these loans by selling minerals.

But these plans were disrupted by the changes in the oil industry in the '70s. As a result, North Korea's economic growth came to a halt. Furthermore, the country started to default in the payment of its loans.

By the mid-1980s, North Korea started to modify its stance on Juche. For the first time since its establishment, it started allowing tourism, foreign investment, and the increase of cooperation with South Korea.

But the situation got worse with the fall of the Soviet Union in 1991. The country withdrew its aid to North Korea and demanded payment for its imports.

The demise of Soviet Union left China as North Korea's biggest helper. Industrial output fell in North Korea in the early

'90s. Consequently, agriculture output also decreased owing to a shortage of fertilizer, pesticides, and electricity.

But the situation got worst in 1994–1998 with a famine that killed at least 3 million people. However, since that famine, North Korea's food supply has increased steadily. It's just that distribution is uneven, leaving some sections of the population with no food.

In 2015, North Korea announced that it was facing the worst drought in the century, sparking fears that the country may go into another famine. Although the fall of North Korea's economy can be attributed to the fall of the Soviet Union and natural disasters, financial mismanagement also played a role: Kim Il-sung's government allegedly wasted money. Adding to this, it devoted a good percentage of its wealth to the military, making weapons it claims to use in defending itself from "US imperialism."

Several sanctions from the UN and other countries also limited North Korea's potential for economic expansion, with only China and South Korea as its biggest trade allies. Apart from tourism and industrialization, the country is also known to fuel its economy by selling weapons to terror organizations and rogue nations.

According to 2013 estimates, North Korea has a population of 24.9 million. And reports indicate that its GDP per capita is $1,800. Comparing this to that of the South, which is $27,513, it's clear that North Korea is among the poorest countries in the world.

Chapter 5: North Korea's Nuclear History

North Korea owes the attention it draws to its nuclear program. Its neighbors, as well as other countries, are on alert watching how far this unpredictable country is willing to go to with its military actions.

But according to North Korea, its nuclear program is only for defense. The series of nuclear bombs tests as well as threats to the USA and South Korea, however, prove that North Korea seriously undermines the threat it raises to global security.

Pyongyang's love for weapons of mass destruction is not new; it has been around for decades. After the war, North

Korea invested heavily in its military. And in 1985, it joined the International Nuclear Non-Proliferation Treaty, which barred it from producing nuclear weapons. Despite that, it established the Yongbyon nuclear reactor in 1986.

The International Atomic Energy Agency accused North Korea of violating the treaty in 1993. And a demand was raised that North Korea must allow inspectors to have access to its nuclear waste storage sites, to which Pyongyang responded with a threat to quit the treaty.

North Korea and the US then signed an agreement in 1994 which forced North Korea to freeze its nuclear program. In return, the US provided heavy fuel and two light-water nuclear reactors to North Korea.

But the world was startled in 1998 when North Korea fired its first long-range missile which flew over Japan and landed in the Pacific Ocean. This brought a lot of tension between the two countries and also placed other neighbors on the edge.

In 2002, USA and its allies halted oil shipment to North Korea after Pyongyang admitted to having been secretly developing a uranium-based nuclear program. USA also named North Korea as part of an "axis of evil," to which the North replied with a threat to the US.

In the same year, North Korea announced that it was reactivating its nuclear facilities at Yongbyon. It also expelled UN inspectors that were installed in the country earlier. This was followed with the withdraw from the International Nuclear Non-Proliferation Treaty in 2003. It also withdrew from a 1992 agreement with South Korea aimed at keeping the peninsula free from nuclear weapons.

As a peaceful solution to the emerging situation, South Korea, China, USA,

Russia, Japan, and North Korea started the six-party talks. North Korea then declared that it had completed the reprocessing of 8,000 spent nuclear fuel rods. And in 2005, it admitted for the first time to have developed nuclear weapons.

In July 2006, it test-fired 7 missiles, including a long-range taepodong-2 missile, which crashed just after take-off. And in October, it conducted the first-ever underground nuclear test.

In response, the UN adopted resolution 1718, imposing economic and commercial sanctions on North Korea. However, following the six-party talks, North Korea closed its main Yongbyon reactor after receiving 50,000 tons of heavy fuel. In addition, its funds that were frozen at a Macau-based bank were released.

This confirmed earlier suspicions many had that North Korea's actions were nothing more than a means of gaining aid.

And this aid would continue with South Korea promising to send 50 million US Dollars to North Korea for flood relief.

Unfortunately, it did not take long before the relationship between the North and South became worse. This was in March 2008 when South Korea elected a new leader, Lee Myung Bak, who promised a harder approach to North Korea.

Later in that year, the US removed North Korea from the terrorism blacklist. And the North agreed to let inspectors have full access to its Yongbyon nuclear site.

However, its relationship with the South remained rocky, with the North declaring all past military and political deals with Seoul nullified in January 2009. Pyongyang accused South Korea of having a hostile intent.

In the following April, North Korea launched a long-range rocket which it claimed was carrying a communications satellite. But its neighbors diffused this claim alleging it was testing long-range missile technology.

The UN Security Council condemned North Korea's actions. And in anger, Pyongyang quit the six-party talks and restated all its nuclear facilities. It then carried out a second underground nuclear test, prompting further condemnation from the UN Security Council.

A North Korean state-run news agency reported in November that the country had reprocessed 8,000 spent fuel rods. This meant it had enough weapons-grade plutonium for one or two nuclear bombs.

In late 2010, rumors surfaced that North Korea had a new secretly-built facility for enriching uranium at its Yongbyon complex. This increased fear in USA, Japan, South Korea, and other countries.

In February 2013, North Korea conducted a third nuclear test claimed to be bigger than the one carried in 2009. This proved that the country's capabilities of making nuclear weapons had reached new heights.

As expected, the UN approved new sanctions on North Korea. In April that year, North Korea restarted all its facilities at its main Yongbyon reactor. This was followed with the launch of 4 short-range missiles in May.

China, which is North Korea's biggest ally, then banned the export of all items that could be used to make missiles or nuclear weapons to North Korea.

In March 2014, North Korea fired two medium-range ballistic missiles after 5 years of not using them. This was followed by several short-range missiles spread all over the year as a sign of anger to the USA and South Korea.

North Korea then placed Yongbyon into operation again in September 2015. This move erased all doubt on whether or not the nuclear reactor was active. The US imposed several new sanctions on North Korea.

In early 2016, it was alleged that North Korea had carried out a fourth underground nuclear test. This was accompanied by several missile fires. The missiles are usually fired during South Korea-US joint military drills. These drills always draw criticism from North Korea, making threats to attack both USA and South Korea if the two don't call off the exercises. Pyongyang calls these exercises as "rehearsals for an invasion."

In light of all this, the word is left with one question – should we be afraid of North Korea? Most experts from USA, which is one country on North Korea's hit list, have varying opinions on North Korea's capabilities of destroying the US.

They claim that North Korea has threatened attacks on the US since the end of the Korean War. And the number of these threats is just too much for anyone to take seriously.

North Korea has made it clear that it will hit the US mainland at any time Washington will force its hand. Despite claiming it has missiles that can hit the US mainland, it has never demonstrated any such abilities.

After the North Korean Cyberattack on Sony Pictures, for example, North Korea threatened to destroy the USA if it tried to retaliate. But it did not destroy the USA.

During the annual joint exercises with South Korea, the USA has never withdrawn and North Korea has never hit the US despite numerous threats.

The worrying thing, however, is that these threats have been increasing. And with reports indicating that North Korea may be expanding its nuclear arsenal, it is normal to have second thoughts.

Worsening the fear was 2010's North Korean shelling of South Korea's Island of Yeonpyeong, which killed 2 marines. The reason for the attack, North Korea claims, was that the South fired in its direction.

But Seoul denied this saying it was conducting annual drills and no fire was aimed in the north. In response to this attack, the South retaliated with 80 missile fires.

The US, UK, EU, UN, and Russia joined voices in condemning North Korea's actions. China maintained a neutral stance urging both sides to do more to contribute to peace. This attack was seen as the greatest since the end of the war. Experts say that North Korea could be on track to building an arsenal of 100 nuclear weapons by 2020.

Chapter 6: Life in North Korea

One would certainly wonder what life is like in North Korea. As information is hard to come by on what happens inside the Hermit kingdom, apart from the propaganda the country broadcasts to the world, we would say we know more about the moon than we do about North Korea.

But there are still a few things we have learned over the years. Those who have visited the country have stories to tell. And defectors also have their own versions.

What Tourists Say

Before going into North Korea, most tourists expect to find an undernourished nation or the police beating people in the streets. However, this is the opposite of what they see.

They find people waking up in the morning to go to work like in any city. Kids are seen in their uniforms rushing to school. And old men have conversations in the sun.

Most tourists swear that the international media feeds them the exact opposite of what life is like in North Korea. And that the horrifying stories told by defectors, or the reports from Human Rights Watch, make one question his or her own existence.

When returning from North Korea, you either believe that Pyongyang is hiding things or that the international media lies to the whole world.

But one thing that's never a doubt is that as a foreigner, you are not allowed much contact with the locals when in North Korea. Furthermore, no matter where you want to go, you always have North Korean tour guides with you.

What Is Life Really Like In North Korea

Defectors agree that the content the North Korean government broadcasts to the world does not correlate with what actually happens in the country. From a young age, North Koreans start consuming propaganda messages around the clock. The messages range from how evil the US is to how the Kims are the best thing that happened to the world.

Concerning the USA, the government tells its people that the US started the Korean War by attacking a peaceful North Korea. The stories go on to detail how the US wanted to take over the whole peninsula but was stopped by the

Great Leader. Unfortunately, the "American imperialists" settled in the South. And now, they rape South Koreans and most of the Koreans on that side are starving to death. If you are in the North, consider yourself lucky.

The messages then change perspective to talk about how great the Kims were, without forgetting the superiority of the Kim of the day. The people of North Korea are told how much their leaders loved and loves them. These messages are on TV, radio, in newspapers, on the streets, etc.

In schools, according to North Korean defectors, 30% of what is taught concerns the Kim Dynasty. Knowing the history of each Kim as well as his achievements is a guarantee for good marks during exams.

Talking about school, most of the kids are forced to participate in mass games when they get in middle school. And some are forced to work for the government.

Despite this, the North Korean government claims that it has a 100% literacy rate.

This fabricated information is made worse by the fact that North Koreans are cut from the rest of the world. Listening to radio stations and watching TV channels not authorized by the state is an offense. The government carries out random checks to ensure that everyone is abiding by this law.

Consumption of foreign media–movies, books, and magazines–is also prohibited. The internet, a thing most of us take for granted, does not exist in North Korea. Only high government officials have access to it, to mainly listening to what the world is saying about the country. The rest of the citizenry has intRAnet, a network comprising of government approved websites.

The government says this tight control on information is to protect the reputation of the West. It fears its citizens may see it as being "unfairly critical to the West."

This control also has its grip on the freedom of religion. Although the North Korean constitution claims people have freedom of worship, anyone doing so does it at his or her own risk. Christianity, for example, is almost non-existent.

Smartphones are slowly becoming widespread in the country, with an estimated 3 million subscribers. However, without the real internet, the phones are mainly limited to making calls and taking pictures. Mostly, people treat these phones as a symbol of how rich one is.

Streets are usually empty as many can't afford cars. But even if they would, traffic would still not be an issue as car ownership is limited to military and high government officials. However, it's not strange to find ordinary people driving cars. Most of these vehicles belong to organizations and are used as if privately owned.

Since the fall of the economy, North Korea has been suffering from electricity problems. Satellite imagery shows that almost the whole of North Korea is in a blackout at night. But apart from the blackouts, it's not many homes that have electricity.

As expected, this issue limits how people can entertain themselves. At night, most entertainment places are closed because of the blackouts. And by 10pm, almost all people are in bed.

Another ridiculous thing is that there are 28 approved haircuts you can choose from. And for men, there are even limits on how long their hair can grow.

Do North Koreans Believe the Government

North Koreans are divided into two: one group buys the stories that the government spreads while another group does not. For example, some tourists claim some locals shout at them that they are dogs or other things. This is a sign of those who believe anyone from the West is evil and to blame for the division of Korea.

But like said, another group knows the government lies to them. This realization has mainly been fueled by the smuggling of movies and other forms of media from China.

Usually, when you go into a market, a vendor will approach you selling local movies. And if he sees that you are open-minded and receptive, he will move on to the restricted stuff. The unfortunate part, however, is that being caught translates into prison time.

Why Don't North Koreans Protest

If North Korea was a democratic country, those fed up with the government would have protested already. Unfortunately, North Korea is a dictatorship. And any form of resistance is rewarded with persecution or execution.

Estimates from the South Korean government and Human Rights Watch indicate that 150,000–200,000 North Koreans are living in prison camps. Those who commit political crimes are sent to the worst camps. The estimates go on to say that about 40% of the prisoners die from malnutrition. Additionally, they are forced to work in mines and farms with inappropriate tools.

The worst part, however, is that with most crimes, you are not the only victim: three of your generations suffer that same fate as you. To avoid such scenarios, parents are known to discipline their kids with force so they don't commit crimes that may affect the whole family.

The government has informants who report those who seem to be opposing. As a result, adversaries have learned to keep their opinions in the confines of their skulls. It is risky to pour your worries even to a best friend. Even in your house, it's hard to trust your own husband or wife with negative matters about the state.

Although some people just disappear (thrown into prison camps), some are taken in broad daylight. This is done on purpose as a lesson to those who may think of opposing.

Defectors say that by the time you may finish making a plan to hold a sit-in, chances are high that you will be in prison before you even get a chance to act.

They also say that they are shocked when they get in other countries and learn there is such a thing as human rights. And because most North Koreans don't know about this, nobody raises a finger about it.

In response to North Korean provocations, South Korea has installed loudspeakers near the border. These broadcast the evils of the North Korean government, mostly to North Korean soldiers. During the day, the messages can be heard from a distance of 10km. And at night, they go as far as 24km.

Defecting

Since it is nearly impossible to protest against the North Korean government, those who do not accept their fate choose to defect, mostly to South Korea.

Despite being illegal, defecting has become a very healthy industry. But getting involved in it means you accept the consequences that come with it: persecution when you get caught. This applies to both the defector and the broker who helps in escaping.

But apart from that, another issue is that the process is expensive. Reports indicate it costs $8,000 to defect to china, which is way too much than what the average North Korean can afford.

In addition, if defecting to South Korea, you need to take a longer route as going directly to the south increases chances of getting caught or being shot. This longer route has a further disadvantage in that it goes through China, where you get sent back if caught.

Most defectors say they are surprised when they reach South Korea and find the citizens there happy. There are no people starving to death. Or anyone being raped by "American imperialists."

The one thing, however, these people miss are the relationships in North Korea. They say people of the North are caring; they share food, enjoy good times together, and more.

This isn't the situation in South Korea where people do not even know the person living next door. Everyone is busy minding his or her own business. Shockingly, some defectors return to North Korea after reaching the South. Considering that defecting is expensive and dangerous, you would think anyone going back is mad.

Analysts have attributed this to the defectors having a hard time fitting in their new world. Most of them are discriminated, leading to unemployment and mental torture. And with gruesome South Korean interrogations, going back home is seen as the best thing.

Others, however, go back in fear of the livelihoods of the relatives left behind. Remember, once your relative is found to have defected, you face persecution. And the brokers who get caught willingly give out the names of people they help defect.

In an effort to reduce defection rates, Kim Jong-un now makes an event of everyone who returns home. He gives him or her $45,000 and a chance to appear on national television. The TV appearance is mainly to show the evils of the country which the defector is coming from and to pronounce how it was a bad idea to defect in the first place.

Furthermore, Kim Jong-un has removed the law which punished defectors after their return to North Korea.

The number of defectors who have reached South Korea is estimated to be 24,000-25,000. While some of these have gone back home, others are believed to be living in China and the West.

Conclusion

I would like to thank for reading the book. And I hope you have learned a lot about North Korea. The one thing this book couldn't reveal, however, is the next move this unpredictable country will make.

Will it really blow up South Korea, USA, and all its allies? Only North Korean officials know.

Will someone rise and challenge the Kim dynasty? That could happen, but it's very unlikely. The closest thing we can expect is that the dynasty will fall on its own. What can facilitate that fall is another matter for debate. And talking about when that can happen, only the future knows.